ANN VOSKAMP

New York Times bestselling author

THE

BROKEN

WAY

a daring path into the abundant life

THE
BROKEN
WAY

Also by Ann Voskamp

The Broken Way: A Daring Path into the Abundant Life

One Thousand Gifts: A Dare to Live Fully Right Where You Are

One Thousand Gifts: A DVD Study: Five Sessions

One Thousand Gifts Devotional: Reflections on Finding Everyday Grace

Selections from One Thousand Gifts: Finding Joy in What Really Matters

The Greatest Gift: Unwrapping the Full Love Story of Christmas

Unwrapping the Greatest Gift: A Family Celebration of Christmas

THE
BROKEN
WAY

A Daring Path into the Abundant Life

STUDY GUIDE

SIX SESSIONS

ANN VOSKAMP

WITH KAREN LEE-THORP

 ZONDERVAN®

ZONDERVAN

The Broken Way Study Guide

Copyright © 2016 by Ann Morton Voskamp

This title is also available as a Zondervan ebook.

ISBN 978-0-310-82074-1

Requests for information should be addressed to:

Zondervan, *3900 Sparks Dr. SE, Grand Rapids, Michigan 49546*

Published in association with William K. Jensen Literary Agency, 119 Brampton Court, Eugene, Oregon 97404.

Cover design: Curt Diepenhorst
Cover photo: Mary Anne Morgan
Interior imagery: PhotoDisc / Siede Preis
Interior design: Kait Lamphere

First Printing October 2016 / Printed in the United States of America

Contents

Read This First

Someone has brought you a bouquet: cornflowers and fragrant freesia. You put them in your favorite vase, a Chinese-patterned porcelain with a graceful swelling around its middle. You turn to take the bouquet to the dining room table, but at that moment one of your children tugs on the hem of your shirt. Startled, you lose your grip on the vase, and it falls. Crashing on the kitchen tile, the vase shatters. Porcelain and flowers litter the floor in a spreading puddle of water. The vase is broken into more than a dozen pieces, broken beyond redemption.

Perhaps that's how you feel: broken beyond redemption. Many of us do. It's a lie. Broken, yes, we are broken, and we won't be fully whole in this lifetime. But beyond redemption, beyond fruitfulness, beyond beauty, beyond an abundant life, no. No human person is so far gone that God can't work in and through us if we let Him.

In fact, brokenness is His chosen way of working through us. God deliberately chooses broken people to be His vessels, and He calls us to be broken and poured out for others. As we follow Him step by step along the road before us, bad brokenness is broken by good brokenness.

So let's sweep up the broken shards of our lives, mop up the water, and breathe a deep draught of the scent of those flowers we've been gifted with. And let's begin taking steps down the surprising road He has laid out for us, the road named the Broken Way.

THE WAY AHEAD

This discussion guide is created to be used in a group of four to ten friends. If you have more than ten people, consider dividing into smaller groups of four to six for your discussion. You want an intimate enough group that even shy people are willing to share their thoughts and talkative people don't dominate. There are cues for the discussion leader at the beginning of each section, so you won't need special training to facilitate the conversation.

This guide contains six sessions to go with six video segments. You can meet weekly for six weeks or at a slower pace if you prefer.

Each session contains these six sections:

- **This Session:** An introduction to the topic you will be exploring in that session.
- **Open Up:** An icebreaker that will help you get to know others in your group while you start discussing the topic.
- **Video Notes:** Key thoughts from the video segment, along with space to write your own notes of what stands out to you in the video.

- **Talk About It:** Questions for your group to discuss. You'll interact with the Bible, the video, and your own stories.
- **Closing Prayer:** A time to share your prayer requests and pray for one another, with special focus on the topic you've been discussing.
- **Between Sessions:** Questions, activities, and journal prompts for you to complete on your own before the next session. Ideally you'll spread these exercises over several sittings rather than trying to do all of them at one time.

For group meetings, each of you will need a copy of this study guide, a pen, a Bible, and an open heart. For the solo work between meetings, you'll need:

- A copy of Ann's book, *The Broken Way: A Daring Path into the Abundant Life* (Zondervan, 2016)
- A pen
- Extra paper or a journal, in case you need more room to express your thoughts

FOR DISCUSSION LEADERS

If your group is sharing the responsibility to lead discussions, assign the six sessions to their respective facilitators up front so that group members can prepare their thoughts and questions before the session they are responsible for leading. Follow the same assignment procedure should your group want to serve any snacks or beverages. Have people volunteer up front to bring refreshments for a given meeting so they know which meeting they are responsible for.

As discussion leader, your primary job is to keep discussions on track with an eye on the clock to be sure you get through the whole session in ninety minutes. You may also need to keep the conversation shared fairly by drawing out quieter members and helping more talkative members to remember that others' insights are valued in your group.

You might find it helpful to preview the session's video teaching segment and then scan the discussion questions that pertain to it, highlighting various questions that you want to be sure to cover during your group's meeting. Ask God in advance of your time together to guide your group's discussion, and then be sensitive to the direction He wishes to lead.

Urge group members to bring their study guide, pen, and a Bible to every gathering. Encourage them to consider buying a copy of *The Broken Way* book by Ann Voskamp to supplement this study.

How Do We Live This One Broken Life?

THIS SESSION

Ask someone to read aloud or summarize the following paragraphs in order to focus the group's thoughts on this session's topic.

Ann's mother was in and out of psychiatric hospitals when Ann was growing up. Ann's sister was accidentally killed by a delivery truck. As a teenager, Ann dealt with the pain of these and other losses by cutting her arms with broken glass. Twenty years later, her skin still bears the scars of that cutting, and her heart still carries sorrow upon sorrow. Life deals out suffering to all of us, and we need to find a way to live in the world unafraid of being broken people.

The good news is that Jesus is on the side of broken people. He went to a cross brokenhearted over the lovelessness of the people He loved, and He let them break His body. If we dare, we can trust Him to heal our bad brokenness with His good brokenness.

This first session gives us a chance to go on record as broken people, to own our brokenness and start moving toward each other and toward God. It's a chance to let some love into the cracks of our broken hearts so that they begin to heal. It's an opportunity to see what Jesus does with His brokenness. Instead of drawing back to protect Himself, He gives thanks, breaks, and gives away what He has to give. The question is, can we become like that?

> "All I can feel is this unspoken brokenness splintering through me. What do you do if you're struggling to remember who you really are? *I'm not enough for any of this.* Not enough for anything I'm doing, for anything I am facing, for anyone I am facing. *Not enough for my life.*"
>
> —*The Broken Way*, page 15

OPEN UP

Give each person up to one minute to respond to the following question. Normally it's not desirable to have everyone answer each question, but for this question at the beginning, everyone should have a chance to respond.

When you look back on the story of your life, tell about a moment when you felt broken. It doesn't have to be your darkest secret, just a time when you were aware that you were flawed.

VIDEO NOTES

View the video segment for session 1. Use the following outline to note anything that stands out to you, any quotes you want to capture, or any responses you have.

How do you live unafraid of broken things?

For a seed to come fully into its own, it must become wholly undone.

Jesus, with His pierced side, is always on the side of the broken.

Despite my fear, I must trust Christ to redeem the broken in me.

Eucharisteo precedes the miracle.

Jesus breaks and gives the bread away.

"My God, my God, why hast thou forsaken me?"

What didn't make the list of graces? The failures.

His love is around us everywhere.

Maybe our hearts are made to be broken. So they can learn to let the love in.

TALK ABOUT IT

Discuss as many of the following questions as time permits. Ask for volunteers to read aloud the Bible passages and the excerpts from Ann's book.

1. What in the video moved you? Is there a line or an image that stands out? Why?

2. Read Psalms 42 and 43. What word pictures does the psalmist use to express his feelings of need and brokenness?

Which of these word pictures speak to your experience? What is it about those that you resonate with?

Verses 42:5, 42:11, and 43:5 repeat the same questions and a determination, all addressed to the psalmist's soul. If you were to ask these same questions of your soul, what might the answers be? Or if these questions don't fit your life right now, what questions would you ask of your soul?

The determination in these three verses is "Put your hope in God, for I will yet praise him, my Savior and my God." How easy is it for you today to put your hope in God? Why?

3. At the Last Supper, Jesus took bread, gave thanks, broke it, and gave it away. What is the bread that Jesus has broken and given to you?

How have you responded? How would you like to respond?

4. In the video, Ann speaks of giving thanks for the brokenness. Can you imagine giving thanks for your brokenness? Why or why not?

"Listen carefully: Unless a grain of wheat is buried in the ground, dead to the world, it is never any more than a grain of wheat. But if it is buried, it sprouts and reproduces itself many times over. In the same way, anyone who holds on to life just as it is destroys that life. But if you let it go, reckless in your love, you'll have it forever, real and eternal."

(John 12:24–25 MSG)

5. Have someone read aloud John 12:24–25 on page 18. In what sense does a planted grain of wheat "die" in order to produce much at harvest time?

How is this like what needs to happen in our lives?

"The paradox of it breaks into me afresh: unless we die, unless we surrender, unless we sacrifice, we remain alone. *Lonely.* But if we die, if we surrender, if we sacrifice, that is when we experience the abundance, that is when we dance in communion. The life that yields the most—yields the most."

—*The Broken Way*, page 41

6. What would it look like for you to die, surrender, sacrifice, or yield in grace and givenness—that is, to live cruciform—in your current situation? Think of one tiny step you could take.

7. In the video, Ann says, "Brokenness happens in a soul so that the power of God can happen in a soul." How have you experienced the power of God in the very place of your brokenness?

8. God is at work, broken and given for you, in the other members of your group. What do you most need from the people in your group? Tell them what would help you—or what *wouldn't* help you if you have a clearer picture of that. Write down what the others in your group say in answer to this question so that you can remember how best to serve, to be broken and given for them in the coming weeks.

"What if the busted and broken hearts could *feel* there's a grace that holds us and calls us Beloved and says we belong and no brokenness ever has the power to break us away from being safe?"

—*The Broken Way*, pages 20–21

CLOSING PRAYER

Have a group member read the following paragraphs aloud. Then let everyone share prayer requests. Finally, take time to pray as a group. It's fine for someone to offer a one-sentence prayer or even to pray silently.

You've probably brought brokenness to this group that you're shy about sharing. You don't want to burden group members with your neediness and risk rejection. The unspoken truth, though, is that we are all broken. And Jesus always stands with the broken, so there is no shame in it. How can the group pray for you at the place of your brokenness? You will honor them if you gift them with a glimpse into your broken heart.

Also, as Ann said in the video, *eucharisteo* or thankfulness always precedes the miracle. In addition to sharing your place of brokenness, share also something you want to thank God for.

As you pray together, begin with thanksgiving, and then move to asking God to enter each person's area of brokenness and transform it over the coming weeks.

Session 1

Work through this section on your own before gathering with your group for session 2. Ideally, spread out the personal study over several sittings.

You probably have much more brokenness in your life than you shared with the group. Wallowing in our limitations isn't helpful, but acknowledging the real things we face is a first step toward dealing with them constructively. This five-part solo work will be about acknowledging what is broken in your life.

MY BROKEN AREAS

Circle the areas listed below where you experience brokenness.

A broken heart   A broken mind

Brokenness of spirit   Brokenness of belief

A broken childhood	Broken-down health
Brokenness of hope	Broken promises
A broken adulthood	Broken-down energy
Broken-down strength	Broken faith
Broken friendships	Broken-down joy

In the box that follows, say more about one of your areas of brokenness. You can journal in words or you can draw a sketch that depicts this broken thing in your life. If you have colored pens, you can choose colors that express your feelings about this broken thing.

Is it helpful for you to express your brokenness instead of keeping it bottled up inside you? How, or why not?

MY THANKFULNESS

"Maybe you can live a full and beautiful life in spite of the great and terrible moments that will happen right inside of you. Actually— maybe you get to *become* more abundant *because* of those moments. . . . Maybe the deepest wounds birth deepest wisdom."

—*The Broken Way*, page 24

What reasons do you have for being thankful in your areas of brokenness? For example, have they given you empathy for Christ's suffering? Have they drawn you to a better understanding of your need for and debt to God? Thankfulness is the key to brokenness that makes you better rather than bitter. Write out your reasons.

Write a thank-you letter to Jesus for the good brokenness He experienced for your sake. Tell Him how He has already made a difference to you in your areas of bad brokenness.

Dear Jesus,

MOVING FORWARD

Maybe up till now you have carried around your brokenness like a backpack full of bricks. It's time to let Jesus unload some of those bricks and put them into His own backpack. In the Bible, the patriarch Jacob wrestled with God all night, and after that night he always walked with a limp. Sometimes God lets us keep a limp as a reminder of our encounter with Him. Sometimes He leaves us with a debilitating or even fatal illness. But often we are carrying around more of a burden than He desires for us. Learning which things He wants to take away and which things He wants us to keep as reminders—that takes time.

What is one area of brokenness in your life that you think God wants you to hand over to Him to heal or transform? Write it here.

_____

Spend some time in silent prayer with your hands held open, offering this issue to God. Allow this sentence to roll around in your mind: "Lover of my soul, I give this to you." If reasons for not letting go of this area of brokenness come to mind, offer those as well. If doubts come to mind about whether you can hand it over to God, give Him those too.

The situation may not be fully fixed in one sitting—God doesn't do magic at our bidding. You may need to offer this issue to Him over and over. If so, do it. To remind yourself that you're being shaped, draw a cross on your wrist or place a cross somewhere you will see it again and again to encourage you to take time each day to lift up your hands and give Him this thing. Additionally, give Him all of your anxieties and frustrations connected with this thing. Brick by brick, hand it all over.

SACRED READING

In each session of this study, you're going to have a chance to reflect on a short passage of Scripture and focus on the transformative journey of living cruciform, broken and given. Take fifteen to twenty minutes each week for this practice to chew on a single passage in a way that fits you best, and consider how your brokenness is shaping you like a cross.

Here is this week's passage:

> For I am poor and needy,
> and my heart is wounded within me.
> I fade away like an evening shadow;
> I am shaken off like a locust.
> *(Psalm 109:22–23)*

This week's passage is intended to bring your brokenness to the surface. You won't be left there, but you do need to start there. This passage is from a type of psalm called a lament. Many of the psalms are laments because the ancient Hebrews thought it was very important to go to God honestly with their brokenness and allow themselves to feel the sadness.

Try to sit with this passage for fifteen to twenty minutes. Where is

God in such a passage? Where does the passage take you? You can do your reflection in any of the following ways:

- You can repeat the passage over and over to yourself, pausing at different words to let them sink in.
- You can pray aloud to God about the passage.
- You can make a sketch that shows what this passage means to you.
- You can journal about the passage, writing about where it takes you and where you find God in it.

As you close your time of reflection, offer a prayer of thanks to God that He is able to handle your honesty about your brokenness and that He doesn't leave you alone in it. Write the prayer here if you'd like.

JOURNAL

Use the space provided to reflect on any of the following topics.

- How you are doing when it comes to letting God take one of the bricks from your backpack.
- How you are doing when it comes to expressing your areas of brokenness so they don't stay bottled up inside you.
- How you might better remind yourself and grow in gratitude for what God is doing in your life.

_____

_____

_____

_____

_____

_____

_____

_____

_____

_____

_____

_____

_____

_____

_____

_____

_____

_____

_____

_____

_____

RECOMMENDED READING

As you reflect on what you have learned in this session, you may want to read the opening section of the book, *The Broken Way* by Ann Voskamp, chapters 1–3. In preparation for session 2, you might want to read chapters 4–6. Jot any highlights in the space below.

Session 2

Living Cruciform

THIS SESSION

Ask someone to read aloud or summarize the following paragraphs in order to focus the group's thoughts on this session's topic.

Seventy years of days adds up to 25,550 days. An average lifespan. A single Mason jar can hold 25,550 kernels of wheat. So few, really, when you think about it.

What will you do with your 25,550 days? Will you spend them trying to distract yourself from the ache of your brokenness? Will you live for a bucket list of fun experiences? Or will you sow those 25,550 grains of wheat, letting them die, letting yourself die to your selfishness, in order to reap a harvest of good for others? This is the question that session 2 asks you to wrestle with: What will you do with the remainder of your 25,550 days?

OPEN UP

Give each person up to one minute to respond to the following question.

What is one thing you want to do before you die?

VIDEO NOTES

View the video segment for session 2. Use the following outline to note anything that stands out to you, any quotes you want to capture, or any responses you have.

I want to trust.

Am I willing to allow God to work through my brokenness?

This bread and wine are symbols of life.

Making your hand reach out, it can be the faith that saves you.

We're all terminal—we all just want a number.

Those who engage in five acts of giving over six weeks are happier.

We exist to be Little Christs.

The magazine editor's bucket list

TALK ABOUT IT

Discuss as many of the following questions as time permits. Ask for volunteers to read aloud the Bible passages and the excerpts from Ann's book.

1. What in the video moved you? Is there a line or an image that stands out? Why?

"When you feel in your marrow how you're His Beloved, you do more than look for signs of His love in the world, more than have a sign of His love; you actually become a sign of His love."

—*The Broken Way*, page 23

2. Read Isaiah 58:6–12. What actions does God list in this passage as examples of the kind of fasting He wants to see us practice?

What results of those habits does God promise in verses 8–12?

How do you respond inwardly to the call of Isaiah 58:6–12? Are you motivated to take action, or are there voices inside you that keep you from wanting to devote energy to these activities? For example, do you think "if I weren't so busy" or "poor people scare me" or "the gospel isn't about doing good works"?

"Learning the art of living is learning the art of giving. . . . The art of giving is believing there is enough love in you, that you are loved enough by Him, to be made enough love to give."

—*The Broken Way*, page 67

3. Read Matthew 25:31–46. What is the difference between the way the sheep live and the way the goats live? What is the eternal destiny of each?

If the sheep are those who are saved by faith in Christ, what would motivate them to exert themselves on behalf of others like this?

4. What opportunities do you have to meet the needs of the suffering around you and "be the gift" to your world? Visit www.thebrokenway .com and brainstorm ideas as a group. Here are some starter ideas (take turns reading them aloud):

- Visit someone you know in a nursing home. Offer to take them on an outing.
- Take a sweet treat to your doctor's office with a note of thanks for being a good doctor.
- Pay for the person behind you at the grocery store.
- Volunteer to be one of the people who visit elderly or sick members of your church who can't get to church. Bring them the Bible readings and your notes on the sermon. Bring them flowers.

- Make a gift bag or plastic bucket for the homeless and keep it in your car until you see someone who needs it. Include new white athletic socks (they're nice and thick), a clean extra-large T-shirt, a toothbrush, toothpaste, soap, deodorant, shampoo, beef jerky, nuts, a gift card to a local fast food restaurant, and anything else you can think of that will stay usable even if it rides around in your car for some days. If it's winter, include a warm hat and some large-sized gloves. When you see a homeless person, give the bucket to him or her.

- Throw a party for your neighbors, especially if you hardly know them. Tape invitations to their doors if that's the only way you know how to contact them.

- Offer to hold someone else's baby during a church service. Or offer to take someone else's toddler out for a run while the parents get to enjoy church in peace. If you don't know the parents well enough, introduce yourself after a service and tell them you'd be happy to help out next week.
  Or if your church has a nursery staffed with approved volunteers, go through the approval process and become a nursery volunteer one Sunday a month.

- Offer to drive someone else's child to an after-school activity.

- Offer to pay the bill for a group at another table in a restaurant. Pay and leave before you have a chance to be thanked, because your reward is in heaven.

- Your ideas:

5. Are there any ideas for giving that you would like to take on—on your own or with others in your group? If so, what are they?

"There is no life worth living without generosity because generosity is a function of abundance mentality. And abundance mentality is a function of identity and intimacy. When you know you are loved enough, that you are made enough, you have abundantly enough to generously give enough. And that moves you into the enoughness of an even more intimate communion."

—*The Broken Way*, pages 68–69

6. What do you think is an "abundance mentality"? How does it differ from a scarcity mentality?

Do you have an abundance mentality and, if so, how are you practicing it? Explain how it, or the lack of it, affects what you do.

7. Why do you suppose doing acts of kindness to be the gift is actually good for you physically and mentally?

8. How are you feeling now about how you want to spend the rest of your 25,550 days?

CLOSING PRAYER

Have a group member read the following paragraphs aloud. Then let everyone share prayer requests. Finally, take time to pray as a group. It's fine for someone to offer a one-sentence prayer or even to pray silently.

If we're not used to doing acts of kindness for others in this way, starting can feel like stepping out onto a rickety wooden bridge. It's awkward, time-consuming, and heart-consuming, but oh so worth it in the end. And all this giving only makes sense if it flows out of how much we have received from God. We live broken and given to others because we have received so much, and we receive so much in the giving. An abundance welling up and overflowing.

What do you want to say to God about choosing to be the gift for others? Tell Him the unvarnished truth if you're scared or eager or full of reservations or stuck in the whirlwind of your life right now. Don't be embarrassed to let the others in your group know what you're feeling.

And if you've come to the group today with needs that want to be laid before the throne of God, crying out for help, then share those now. Or if you're overflowing with gratitude for some answered prayer, speak out your gratitude so that everyone in the group can share the celebration. How can the group pray for you? What do you need in order to be able to pursue daily cruciformity and live poured out for others?

BETWEEN SESSIONS

Session 2

Work through this section on your own before gathering with your group for session 3. Ideally, spread out the personal study over several sittings.

Maybe doing good things for others is already a habit as familiar as breathing for you. If you have small children, being broken and given for others may be all you do all day long. Or maybe the idea of spending the rest of your 25,550 days giving your life for others has smacked you in the face and left you reeling. Either way, you're right where God wants to work with you. This session's solo work will give you a chance to plan, do, and reflect on an act of kindness for others and experience a deeper union with Christ in all you suffer and give.

MY PLAN

"What if instead of waiting for good enough things to happen to us, we could be the good thing to happen to someone else who's waiting? What if we could cure our own waiting room addiction by making room in our life to be the good others are waiting for?"

—*The Broken Way*, pages 87–88

Who have been the models and mentors in your life—past or present—who have demonstrated to you how to break and give your life for the suffering of others? List at least a few.

-
-
-
-
-

Do you think you can do it the way they do it, or is your personality such that you need to find a different way of sharing communion in suffering and expressing generosity? Explain.

Question 4 of the group discussion offered some ideas for doing an act of kindness (see pages 37–39). What practical act of living cruciform will you choose to be the gift for others this week?

What materials will you need to assemble? What help, if any, do you need?

When will you do it? Put your plan on your calendar.

"Maybe there's no such thing as a small act of giving. Every small gift of grace creates a love quake that has no logical end. It will go to the ends of the earth and change the world and then it will break through time and run on into eternity."

—*The Broken Way*, page 73

MY REFLECTIONS ON WHAT HAPPENED

Go out and be the gift! Then come back and write about what it was like for you. What happened? How do you feel as a result? What are your thoughts about doing this kind of thing again? Use the space below or your own journal to debrief the experience of being broken and given. Also consider sharing your experience at www.thebrokenway.com and on your social media sites using the #betheGIFT hashtag.

Did something get in the way of your following through and doing what you planned? If so, describe what happened. Are you going to do the same thing next week, or adjust to better meet others' deeper needs? If the latter is the case, what will you do?

SACRED READING

This week you will once again get to reflect on a short passage of Scripture that encourages you in the transformative journey of living cruciform, broken and given, for deeper abundance. Take fifteen to twenty minutes to chew on this one passage, and again choose a way of reflection that fits you best.

Here is this week's passage:

> Hear me, LORD, and answer me,
>   for I am poor and needy.
> Guard my life, for I am faithful to you;
>   save your servant who trusts in you.
> You are my God; have mercy on me, Lord,
>   for I call to you all day long.
>
> *(Psalm 86:1–3)*

In this week's passage we continue to confess that we are poor and needy, but we take a next step. Where does the psalmist go that is new? How is this a good response to brokenness? Where is God in this passage? Where are you?

Try to sit with this passage for fifteen to twenty minutes. You can do your reflection in any of the following ways:

- You can repeat the passage over and over to yourself, pausing at different words to let them sink in.

- You can pray aloud to God about the passage.
- You can make a sketch that shows what this passage means to you.
- You can journal about the passage, writing about where it takes you and where you find God in it.

As you close your time of reflection, offer a prayer of thanks to God that He understands your needs and hears your cries for mercy. Write your prayer below if you'd like.

RECOMMENDED READING

In preparation for session 3, you might want to read chapters 7, 8, and 14 of *The Broken Way*. Jot any highlights in the space below.

Learning to Receive

THIS SESSION

Ask someone to read aloud or summarize the following paragraphs in order to focus the group's thoughts on this session's topic.

Living given, pouring yourself out for other people, is the best way to deal with brokenness. But acts of kindness should never be done out of pressure to perform, out of "a cacophony of voices about who you should be or how you are supposed to feel or how you have to do this and that and this to be good enough," as Ann puts it. Instead, giving is always, always preceded by receiving from God in union with Him. And for many of us receiving in humility is far harder than giving. Giving can make us feel powerful, in control, while receiving makes us vulnerable.

Yet receiving in communion, koinonia, is where it all starts. We start by receiving life from God when we're nothing but a few cells united to our mother in her womb. We receive our identity as beloved children made in God's image and remade in Christ's likeness. We receive all of our physical needs from the adults in our world until we're old enough to start feeding and clothing ourselves. Along the way, people mess up and we get broken, yet we continue to receive not in spite of our brokenness but in the midst of it.

This session is about learning to receive *in communion*—to receive identity from Christ and love from God through people. It's a chance to exhale and live without the pressure to do anything to deserve it. Lean back. Breathe. Let God minister to your thirsty soul with the relief of deep intimacy.

"Letting yourself be loved is an act of terrifying vulnerability and surrender. Letting yourself be loved is its own kind of givenness. Letting yourself be loved gives you over to someone's mercy and leaves you trusting that they will keep loving you, that they will love you the way you want to be loved, that they won't break your given heart."

—*The Broken Way*, page 100

OPEN UP

Give each person up to one minute to respond to the following question.

If you pursued meeting someone's brokenness this week, you lived broken and given. Tell what you learned. Don't tell what you did (it's best to keep those things private), but do tell what you learned from the experience.

Then share this with the group: Is it easier for you to give to others or to receive from others? Why? (If neither is easy for you, talk about why.)

VIDEO NOTES

View the video segment for session 3. Use the following outline to note anything that stands out to you, any quotes you want to capture, or any responses you have.

The Farmer's foot massage

Why does it sometimes feel better to give than to receive?

Everywhere, the possibility of a vulnerable communion

Grace enough to grow you toward transformation

We first receive, so that we have something to give.

Let feelings be fully felt and then fully surrendered to God.

Identity in Christ

Self-lies

TALK ABOUT IT

Discuss as many of the following questions as time permits. Ask for volunteers to read aloud the Bible passages and the excerpts from Ann's book.

1. What in the video moved you? Is there a line or an image that stands out? Why?

2. Read John 8:2–11. How easy is it for you to identify with the woman caught in adultery? Why?

Notice what Jesus says to the woman in verse 11. Do His words invite division or deeper communion? Explain.

Why is it important that He releases her from condemnation before He says, "Go and leave your life of sin"? How would it be different if He said, "Go and leave your life of sin. Then I won't condemn you"?

3. Do you ever feel as if you need to clean up your life of sin before Jesus releases you from condemnation? And yet doesn't Jesus continually demonstrate koinonia in the Gospels, a willingness to share in our suffering and brokenness? Why do you suppose we still often feel condemned instead of free to receive mercy?

"It is your intimacy with Christ that gives you your identity. You can't experience the power of Christ, the mission of Christ, being made new in Christ, until you know who you are in Christ. Your identity literally means "the same"—that regardless of changing circumstances, the core of you is unchangeable, stable, the same."

—*The Broken Way*, page 185

4. Ann says, "You can't experience intimacy with Christ until you know your identity in Christ." Choose *one* of the biblical descriptions of your identity below, and tell how you do or don't relate to it as being true about you. What helps you or gets in the way?

- "God's chosen people, holy and dearly loved" (Colossians 3:12)
- "holy and blameless in his sight" (Ephesians 1:4)
- "So you are no longer a slave, but God's child; and since you are his child, God has made you also an heir." (Galatians 4:7)

5. How do you react to Ann's words quoted below? What would you do if you knew you were brave enough, strong enough, *enough* enough because Christ in you is enough?

"You aren't your yesterday, you aren't your messes, you aren't your failures, you aren't your brokenness. You are brave enough for today, because He is. You are strong enough for what's coming, because He is. And you are enough for all that is, *because He always is*."

—*The Broken Way*, page 185

6. How do the people in your group receive reminders that they're loved unconditionally? How do they continue to believe it? How have others helped you?

"What if you just want desperately, in spite of everything, for someone to remember how hard you've really tried? There are days when the sharp edge of self-condemnation cuts you so deep that you can be reaching, grasping, but can't seem to remember to believe that He believes in you."

—*The Broken Way*, page 181

CLOSING PRAYER

Have a group member read the following paragraphs aloud. Then let everyone share prayer requests. Finally, take time to pray as a group. It's fine for someone to offer a one-sentence prayer or even to pray silently.

One way you can receive and pursue communion with others is to let yourself be prayed for. To give everyone enough time to be prayed for, divide into subgroups of three to five people. Tell your subgroup the struggles and even sufferings in your life right now.

When you pray for someone in your subgroup, place a hand on that person's shoulder so that he or she can physically feel the connection between you. In this way, you are learning to practice being shaped by others' sufferings.

Session 3

Work through this section on your own before gathering with your group for session 4. Ideally, spread out the personal study over several sittings.

This session's solo work is about solidifying your sense of identity in Christ. If writing isn't the mode of expression you prefer, try speaking aloud or drawing. Play around with different modes until you identify what penetrates your defenses most effectively.

MY IDENTITY

Choose one of these three identity statements you talked about as a group in question 4 (page 56).

- "God's chosen people, holy and dearly loved" (Colossians 3:12)
- "holy and blameless in his sight" (Ephesians 1:4)

- "So you are no longer a slave, but God's child; and since you are his child, God has made you also an heir." (Galatians 4:7)

Rephrase it here as a statement about who you are:

Take five to ten minutes to chew on this statement—just that, nothing else—so that it sinks into your soul. You can sit quietly and repeat it over and over in your mind, or you can write it out over and over, or you can journal about what it signifies for you, or draw a picture of it—whatever works best for you to let something soak in.

How effective was this form of reflection in helping you remember God's love for you? Chances are that five minutes of reflection won't magically shift your heart into deeply believing it, since it has been a challenge for years. But do this reflection every day this week for five or ten minutes, and also during your morning commute if that's your best time. If distractions come (and they will), just gently keep setting them aside and get back to the truth. Don't beat yourself up for getting distracted. Settled attention is a skill that has to be practiced in order to improve. And remember, your efforts to pursue union with Christ by sharing in His sufferings and the world's is also forming your identity day by day. Here's some space for any additional thoughts or pictures.

A PRAYER TO GOD

In the box that follows, write a prayer to God confessing any doubts you have had about His love for you or the reality that, apart from Christ in you, you're not in and of yourself brave enough, strong enough, or holy enough for Him. What do you want to say to God about your union with Him and your identity through Him?

Dear God,

Now write God's response. If you need help, look at Romans 8:31–39.

Dear Child of Mine,

GIVING AND RECEIVING

Make time for coffee or a meal with a close friend or spouse to practice surrender by giving and receiving comfort for your struggles. Share and ask about any areas of brokenness or suffering as a way to practically pursue being "shaped by cruciformity" in communion together. It doesn't need to be formal or structured; simply share the things you are struggling with and practice listening to their struggles and not offering answers. Affirm the importance of their experience, your appreciation of their willingness to help you, and who you and they are in Christ. Afterward, come back to this space and write about how the time went.

SACRED READING

This week you will once again get to reflect on a short passage of Scripture that takes you on the journey from brokenness to abundance. Take fifteen to twenty minutes to chew on this passage:

> I waited patiently for the LORD;
>> he turned to me and heard my cry.

He lifted me out of the slimy pit,

out of the mud and mire;

he set my feet on a rock

and gave me a firm place to stand.

(Psalm 40:1–2)

Can you truthfully say that God has lifted you out of the slimy pit? Has He set your feet on a firm place? Maybe you're in the process of being lifted out and it's taking longer than you'd like. Maybe your identity statement is part of that process. Where are you and God in the process of your rescue from bad brokenness?

You can do your reflection in any of the following ways:

- You can repeat the passage over and over to yourself, pausing at different words to let them sink in.
- You can pray aloud to God about the passage.
- You can make a drawing that shows what this passage means to you.
- You can journal about the passage, writing about where it takes you and where you find God in it.

As you close your time of reflection, thank God that He has heard your cry and is in the process of setting you on solid rock. Write your prayer below if you'd like.

RECOMMENDED READING

In preparation for session 4, you might want to read chapters 9–12 of *The Broken Way*. Jot any highlights in the space below.

Real Koinonia

THIS SESSION

Ask someone to read aloud or summarize the following paragraphs in order to focus the group's thoughts on this session's topic.

In the story *The Velveteen Rabbit*, a toy rabbit longs to become real. Another stuffed animal tells him that toys become real when a child has loved them for a long time. Often this process of love causes the toy to be worn down and damaged, but the pain of that doesn't matter because becoming real is so wondrous.

This story, written in 1922, has been treasured by generations of readers because it expresses truths we know deep down: that love is what makes us real, and that becoming real is worth any amount of pain.

In this session, we'll listen past the regrets that haunt our quiet moments and the lies Satan tries to tell us about ourselves to hear the voice of God telling us that the Broken Way is the way to become real.

"What seems to be undoing you can ultimately remake you. *What if the deeper you know your own brokenness, the deeper you can experience your own belovedness?* I wonder if this is the refrain of the believing life: I fall because I am broken . . . but I always rise because I am always beloved . . . ?"

—*The Broken Way*, pages 146–147

OPEN UP

Give each person up to one minute to respond to the following question.

Do you have any regrets, anything about your past that you would do over if you could? Finish this sentence: "If only . . ."

VIDEO NOTES

View the video segment for session 4. Use the following outline to note anything that stands out to you, any quotes you want to capture, or any responses you have.

Regret for what won't ever be

Satan's lies

What's real is our untouchable worth in Christ to God.

Becoming real

Cutting Joshua's hair

TALK ABOUT IT

Discuss as many of the following questions as time permits. Ask for volunteers to read aloud the Bible passages and the excerpts from Ann's book.

1. What in the video moved you? Is there a line or an image that stands out? Why?

2. Ann says, "What's real is our untouchable worth in Christ to God." Is that truth any more real to you after reflecting on your identity in the between-sessions homework? Talk about what was helpful to you (or not) in the solo work.

3. The apostle Paul says, "Forgetting what is behind and straining toward what is ahead, I press on toward the goal to win the prize for which God has called me heavenward in Christ Jesus" (Philippians 3:13–14). What are some things behind you that it might be best to forget?

Are regrets ever good for us to remember? If so, which ones? If not, why not?

"What is real? Real living, real believing, real faith? Real living doesn't always feel like living; it can feel like you're dying. It can feel like you are breaking apart and losing pieces of yourself—and you are. Because when you let yourself love, you let parts of you die. *Or you aren't really loving.* You must let your false self be broken, parts of you that you only thought were necessary. You must embrace your union with Christ, bravely surrender and trust that what's breaking and being lost is never the eternal, needed parts of you, but always the temporal, needless parts that were getting in the way of you becoming real."

—*The Broken Way*, page 148

4. Read Ann's words above. Do you ever feel like you are breaking apart and losing pieces of yourself? How can that be a constructive process?

"Anyone who intends to come with me has to let me lead. You're not in the driver's seat; *I* am. Don't run from suffering; embrace it. Follow me and I'll show you how. Self-help is no help at all. Self-sacrifice is the way, my way, to saving yourself, your true self. What good would it do to get everything you want and lose you, the real you?"

(Mark 8:34–37 MSG)

5. Read Mark 8:34–37 above. Practically, how are you embracing suffering in your life right now? Specifically, how are you not running but instead embracing suffering and brokenness in any key areas of your life?

How could self-sacrifice be the way to saving your true self?

6. Ann says, "Let your suffering create love." What does that mean? How can you do that?

"Every to-do list can be a to-love list."

—*The Broken Way*, page 108

7. How can we turn our to-do list into a to-love list? What thing on your to-do list do you most need to see as really a way of loving Jesus and someone in your life?

"You are the most loved not when you're pretending to have it all together; you are actually the most loved when you feel broken and falling apart."

—*The Broken Way*, page 150

CLOSING PRAYER

Have a group member read the following paragraphs aloud; they're written in the form of a prayer. Then let everyone share prayer requests. Finally, take time to pray as a group. It's fine for someone to offer a one-sentence prayer or even to pray silently.

O Lord God, we want our suffering to create love, not bitterness or despair. We need strength from You to choose this hour by hour. We need Your help to recognize the opportunities to choose love and to see Your face in others.

We want so much to be real and forget regrets that hold us back. We don't want to present a false face to the world but to see all the falseness chipped away, even if that hurts. Please help us to endure the process of becoming real, and to find true communion more and more in believing that we are loved in our brokenness. Thank You for what You're doing in each one of us.

Session 4

Work through this section on your own before gathering with your group for session 5. Ideally, spread out the personal study over several sittings.

Your solo time this week will be invested in practices that will help you engage in koinonia and become real. You're going to talk back to your inner critic, try out a to-love list, get some guidance from someone who might be a mentor to you, and continue your practice of sacred reading. These are four practices that you could make into habits for seeking real koinonia.

"This is the thing: the prosecutor of your soul can't ever nail you. Time can't wreck your life. *You* can't wreck your life. Nothing in all this world can separate you from the love of Christ, and His love is your life. Your life is *unwreckable*. Because Christ's love is unstoppable."

—*The Broken Way*, page 146

CALMING THE INNER CRITIC

We all have an inner critic, a voice inside that wrongly equates what we do with who we are. This is not the voice of conscience, the Holy Spirit who convicts of selfishness and pride. This is always a critical voice that's unreasonably harsh, the one Ann talks about that says we're a failure, damaged goods. It makes no distinction between *how we do* and *who we are*. It paints us as all bad.

Write down some of the things your inner critic says about you. If it criticizes your work, write that down. If it criticizes your appearance, write that down. If it criticizes your parenting or housekeeping or anything else, write it down.

-
-
-
-
-
-

Read Romans 8:1. How is this relevant to what your inner critic says about you?

Read Romans 8:31–39. What statements in this passage most directly contradict what your inner critic says about you?

Now write the honest truth that God would say in response to each of your critic's attacks. For example, "To the people who really love me, I am a beautiful human being. They don't care how old I am or how much I weigh." "Nothing can separate me from the love of Christ." "There is now no condemnation for those who are in Christ Jesus." "God is good enough to turn around the bad broken in me and make me a person who loves." "I am of incalculable worth to God."

-
-
-
-
-
-

Copy these positive statements onto 3 x 5 cards or turn them into text messages to yourself. Read them aloud three times a day for the next week. The goal here is to replace the lies of the inner critic with the truth of God, with the identity of who you are in Him because of union with Him.

MENTORING TIME

Email or talk face-to-face with someone who is a good model of being real in the midst of brokenness. Ask them what their secret is. Do they think about how much it costs them to live like that? (I bet they don't.) Ask them if they've always been that way. Who modeled this way of life for them? Tell them what you see them doing, and ask them to pray for you to become more like that.

Use the space that follows to jot down some takeaways from your interaction.

TO-LOVE LIST

Make a to-love list. Write down what you need to do and how it will express love to someone. The list can be simple chores such as laundry and cleaning the bathtub, or more creative ideas such as the "be the gift" acts of kindness you contemplated in session 2 (visiting someone in a nursing home, paying for someone behind you in the grocery store, making a gift bucket for the homeless, etc.).

To-Love List

What I'm Going to Do	How It Will Express Love

Once you've done most of the items on your to-love list, come back to the study guide and write about the experience in the space provided on the next page. How was it like or unlike doing items on a to-do list? Is it hard for you to think of these activities as seeking koinonia love in action? Why or why not? How might you feel and experience more of the abundance of God if you saw your to-do list as a way of living more into koinonia, communion?

SACRED READING

You've reflected on your poverty. You've cried out to God. You've entered into the process of being rescued from the mud. This week you're going to think about hope. Take fifteen to twenty minutes to chew on this passage:

> Show me your ways, LORD,
>   teach me your paths.
> Guide me in your truth and teach me,
>   for you are God my Savior,
>   and my hope is in you all day long.
>
> *(Psalm 25:4–5)*

Who is God in this passage? What is hope? Can you hope in God even if you're still broken? What are you asking for in this passage? What does it have to do with the journey toward abundance?

Try to sit with this passage for fifteen to twenty minutes. You can do your reflection in any of the following ways:

- You can repeat the passage over and over to yourself, pausing at different words to let them sink in.
- You can pray aloud to God about the passage.
- You can make a sketch that shows what this passage means to you.
- You can journal about the passage, writing about where it takes you and where you find God in it.

As you close your time of reflection, offer a prayer of thanks to God that He is your Savior and is guiding you toward truth. Write your prayer below if you'd like.

RECOMMENDED READING

In preparation for session 5, you might want to read chapters 13 and 15 of *The Broken Way.* Jot any highlights in the space below.

Embracing
Inconvenience

THIS SESSION

Ask someone to read aloud or summarize the following paragraphs in order to focus the group's thoughts on this session's topic.

Long before we are healed of our brokenness, God invites us to see our own pain mirrored in the pain-struck faces of others. We know what it is to be thirsty, so we read the thirst in the other person's eyes. We know what it's like to need help, so we're eager to offer help to another. We stretch ourselves on behalf of neighbors and even strangers, knowing that the biblical word for *hospitality* means "love of strangers."

This session will take us more deeply into the unpredictable but holy place of other people's pain. We care about this pain not in spite of the fact that we have plenty of our own pain, but because we have plenty of our own. In this session we will consider what each of us, limited as we are, can do to love broken others as God loves us in our brokenness.

"Love of strangers—wasn't that the direct, exact translation of the word for hospitality in Scripture, *philoxenia*? *Philos*—brotherly love; *xenia*—the stranger. Love the stranger like a brother. Biblical hospitality is about inviting strangers in, not just the neighbors."

—*The Broken Way*, page 204

OPEN UP

Give each person up to one minute to respond to the following question.

When in your life has someone gone out of his or her way to help you or to be with you in your pain?

VIDEO NOTES

View the video segment for session 5. Use the following outline to note anything that stands out to you, any quotes you want to capture, or any responses you have.

Gordon

Cutting

Elizabeth

We embrace others' brokenness because Jesus does.

Courageous enough to let the Gordons break into us

There's always enough room at our tables for those in need.

Elizabeth and the brownie bucket

Help when it's not convenient

TALK ABOUT IT

Discuss as many of the following questions as time permits. Ask for volunteers to read aloud the Bible passages and the excerpts from Ann's book.

1. What in the video moved you? Is there a line or an image that stands out? Why?

2. Read Luke 14:12–14. What does Jesus tell His followers to do in this passage? Why?

   How do these verses affect your views on surrendering to givenness, especially with the poor and disabled?

What is difficult about choosing to practice what Jesus teaches here? Why exactly is it difficult?

"'Yeah, Gordon.' The words spill out before I'm really thinking, trying to get the invitation out before reservations. 'We've got an extra bed up in the loft . . .' I could hear the cautions in my head: Is this safe? *But what is love if not this? Real love is never safe.* When it comes to real love, there is safety in danger. How many times have I thought it was safety that mattered, when Jesus already died to save us? No one ever got saved unless someone else was willing to be unsafe. Some notion of safety isn't what ultimately matters; what matters is: *If we see someone in need and don't help in some way, isn't that in some way sin?*"

—*The Broken Way*, pages 202, 204

3. How do you respond to Ann's words above? How can you more easily choose to be the gift and help others even when it's inconvenient? Are you working on being more willing to help and share yourself when it's risky? Why or why not?

4. Read Luke 10:29–37. How do the Samaritan's actions reveal him being "broken bread given away" here?

How do you feel when you think of Jesus asking you to "Go and do likewise" (verse 37)? Do you think our familiarity with personal suffering has anything to do with our willingness or lack thereof?

5. Why do you suppose this isn't the way most Christians live?

"Love is the willingness to be interrupted. *Interrupt* comes from the Latin word *interrumpere*, meaning "break into." *Love is the willingness to be broken into.* There are never interruptions in a day—only manifestations of Christ."

—*The Broken Way*, page 177

6. How would your life be different if you thought of every seeming interruption as a manifestation of Christ, a big or small opportunity to enter into participation in His sufferings? What is one way this week you want to not be afraid of brokenness and participate in the sufferings of Christ, having deeper koinonia with Him and your world?

7. This session has dealt with one of the hardest challenges Jesus places before us. For most of us, the teaching here leads far outside our comfort zones. Some of us have a higher tolerance for risk than others, but what is a step—even a small one—that you could take to show hospitality toward those in need? Or what could your group do? What such outreaches are already happening through your church?

CLOSING PRAYER

Have a group member read the following paragraphs aloud. Then let everyone share prayer requests. Finally, take time to pray as a group. It's fine for someone to offer a one-sentence prayer or even to pray silently.

Most of us are too afraid or too preoccupied to love other broken people to the extent that Ann describes. But if we really recognize ourselves as broken people, then we won't have an us-and-them mentality that puts people in need on the other side of a wall from us. We'll break down that wall and see the poor, the homeless, and the disabled as fundamentally like us. Many of the homeless are mentally ill or drug-addicted or both, but they are still human beings created in the image of God who are trying to cope with the hand life has dealt them. The disabled aren't defined by their disability any more than we are defined by our brokenness; they have remarkable gifts just as all of us do.

Let your prayers today concentrate on the needs of others and on your own need to see your place in loving them. You can't do everything, but pray to discern something you *can* do to be the gift and live broken and given.

Session 5

Work through this section on your own before gathering with your group for session 5. Ideally, spread out the personal study over several sittings.

This week's solo time will be devoted mainly to two projects: research on what can be done to help and offer yourself to those in need, and prayer to open your heart to the needs around you. The goal is to broaden your thinking and empathy so that you see ways to offer practical love and koinonia. You'll also continue to do sacred reading on the topic of giving.

RESEARCH

Spend some time on the Internet researching ways to help those in need. For example, visit www.thebrokenway.com for resources on how to be the gift. This will help you get past the false notion that nothing can be done safely and effectively.

One idea is to run an Internet search of "shower facilities for the homeless." That will turn up places around the country where these services are being offered. If there isn't one near you, you can contact a more distant ministry and find out how they went about setting up their program and what advice they have for you.

Also, find out what organizations are already dealing with the homeless and needy in your area. There may be an existing ministry that provides beds, showers, or laundry facilities, for example. Find out how you can contribute your time and/or money to these endeavors. Ask for advice from the professionals, and listen to them closely. You haven't committed to doing anything yet; you are just gathering information.

As well, find out what your church is already doing. You may be surprised that more goes on in a quiet way than you expected. People in need often contact pastors or church offices for help, and your pastor might be happy to know that your group is investigating ways to help people. Who in your church would be a good contact person to educate you on what the church is doing or what volunteers can contribute? Who in your church might know what other organizations in your community (food banks, clothing banks, soup kitchens, transitional housing ministries, etc.) are active?

Your local schools are also a resource. The principal's office or school counselor may know of disadvantaged children who attend their school. You can offer to buy school supplies or clothing knowing only the ages of the children, not their names. The recipients won't get your name either. The gift is completely anonymous to protect everyone's privacy, but you can know it's going to a child or family who really needs it.

On an international level, organizations such as Compassion International and World Vision are worth investigating. Find out how individuals, families, and small groups can contribute to what they do and share online with #betheGIFT hashtag.

Take notes about what you learn here:

HEART EXERCISE

Hopefully, some of that research has gotten you excited about pursuing the practice of cruciformity in your community. But you will likely still have concerns or questions about how to start. Write your questions and concerns here.

Write a letter to God, telling Him candidly what you're thinking about reaching your hand out to other broken people. Tell Him your fears about sharing in others' sufferings. Thank Him for the resources He has given you, and tell Him how you struggle with sharing them. If your life feels more like it's about scarcity than abundance right now, say so. Be completely honest.

Dear God,

What do you hear God saying back to you?

Dear Child of Mine,

"This is all I can do now to try to keep loving her: I can show up. Elizabeth would have loved that. Would she have loved it if I had showed up more? Showed up with the gift of an old frayed blanket and told her—not asked her, but told her—that we were going to the park with a stack of old books to watch the clouds? If I had called her back that time I thought it was too late? If I hadn't walked by that scarf that was screaming her name and surprised her with it as a just-because gift? If I'd stolen five minutes, grabbed a postcard, and scrawled out three lines—'There isn't a laugh in the world like yours. You handed me a life supply of courage because you loved me like this. And yeah, you pretty much beat me at everything, but I win at this: I love you more.' Why hadn't I been that gift more often? The ministry of presence is a gift with an expiry date."

—*The Broken Way*, pages 165–166

Maybe you don't need a big plan or an organization right now. Maybe you already know a person in need who could benefit from your friendship. If so, who is that person? How can you extend yourself for him or her?

After all this research and prayer, what is a step you can take forward? Maybe you have an idea that your group can do, or maybe you have an idea that you or your family can do. Write down one small step forward that you can take to be generous and practice hospitality and koinonia.

SACRED READING

You've asked God to teach you His paths, and you've cast your hope on Him. One of His most important principles is about being generous with others even in our own need, so this week's passage will allow you to reflect on that. Take fifteen to twenty minutes to chew on it:

"Give, and it will be given to you. A good measure, pressed down, shaken together and running over, will be poured into your lap. For with the measure you use, it will be measured to you."

(Luke 6:38)

These are words of Jesus. How are they true? How could they be twisted or abused? Picture in your mind the measure you tend to use for giving to people. How big is it? Why? What would you like your measuring scoop to look like?

Try to sit with this passage for fifteen to twenty minutes. You can do your reflection in any of the following ways:

- You can repeat the passage over and over to yourself, pausing at different words to let them sink in.
- You can pray aloud to God about the passage.
- You can make a sketch that shows what this passage means to you.
- You can journal about the passage, writing about where it takes you and where you find God in it.

As you close your time of reflection, offer a prayer of thanks to God that He is eager to give you a good measure, overflowing. Write your prayer below if you'd like.

RECOMMENDED READING

In preparation for session 6, you might want to read chapters 16–18 of *The Broken Way*. Jot any highlights in the space below.

Who We Serve

THIS SESSION

Ask someone to read aloud or summarize the following paragraphs in order to focus the group's thoughts on this session's topic.

Koinonia communion—the vital connection with God and others that gives us our very life—can happen only when we're broken and given. So brokenness isn't something we get over when we reach some stage of healing; it's an ongoing experience for all of this life. As we come to the end of this study, we're not focused on giving to others out of our strength but out of our weakness and need. Serving others in our need is the most loving gift we can give them, and how we find ourselves served by God. *Compassion* means "to suffer with," and the more we travel down the Broken Way, the more we are willing to suffer with others and to let them suffer with us.

In this final session, Ann shares some of her own anxieties and mistakes so that we can feel safe to share our anxieties and mistakes with our trusted others. Perhaps surprisingly, vulnerably sharing our failures and fears can be an act of service taking us deeper into communion with God and one another. The Broken Way is Jesus' way of being in the world, so it will be our ongoing way as we go forward beyond this group. We don't have to live in fear of broken things because Christ is redeeming everything.

OPEN UP

Give each person up to one minute to respond to the following question.

Describe a time when you felt deeply connected to another person, deeply loved by them. What happened to make you feel this way? Did this person know about your broken areas? Whether yes or no, how did that affect the connection?

VIDEO NOTES

View the video segment for session 6. Use the following outline to note anything that stands out to you, any quotes you want to capture, or any responses you have.

Kai's diabetes

Coming home to wet laundry and oozing trash

Opening an anxious heart to friend Mei

Creating communities around suffering

A walk with Hope

TALK ABOUT IT

Discuss as many of the following questions as time permits. Ask for volunteers to read aloud the Bible passages and the excerpts from Ann's book.

1. What in the video moved you? Is there a line or an image that stands out? Why?

"Why not embrace the life work of embracing suffering, embracing brokenness? Why avoid the gift of more God, more vulnerability, more intimacy, more communion—the gifts that brokenheartedness offers? Why had I found that terrifying to incarnate? Suffering is a call for presence; it's a call for us to be present—not only to the brokenness in the world, but to the brokenness in our own soul, and to risk trusting others with our wounds."

—*The Broken Way*, page 255

2. How are you internally broken? What psychological scars, emotional baggage, or personal issues have you not shared with your group? Offer your brokenness to the group, because sharing among trusted friends is where deep koinonia communion will come from. (Remember, confidentiality is key here. What is shared in the group stays in the group. And if prayer seems appropriate during this time of sharing, pause to do so.)

"Sometimes, it's more than being afraid of any broken things—we're afraid to be a burden to anyone. Sometimes—we just can't bear the thought that our brokenness might break anyone else. Sometimes—it seems easier to bury our hurt than break anyone's heart."

—*The Broken Way*, pages 247–248

3. What is it like for you to hear others share their brokenness? Does it draw you closer to them or push you away? Are you afraid to be seen as weak but see others who share weakness as brave? Why is that, do you think? How are you practicing every day to live unafraid of brokenness?

4. We give to others out of our brokenness. Share what you learned after applying the practical ideas in session 5 about helping others in need. Did you learn anything you can share that might help the group in their practice of daily finding opportunities to be shaped like a cross?

We continue to shout our praise even when we're hemmed in with troubles, because we know how troubles can develop passionate patience in us, and how that patience in turn forges the tempered steel of virtue, keeping us alert for whatever God will do next. In alert expectancy such as this, we're never left feeling shortchanged. Quite the contrary—we can't round up enough containers to hold everything God generously pours into our lives through the Holy Spirit!

(Romans 5:3–5 MSG)

5. Read Romans 5:3–5 above. What do you think passionate patience looks like in action? (Other translations use the word *endurance* or *perseverance*.)

Have you experienced troubles producing passionate patience, virtue (character), and alert expectancy (hope) in you? Or have you seen yourself or others grow in passionate patience, virtue, and alert expectancy as a result of suffering? Talk about what you have seen or experienced.

"Suffering is not a problem that needs a *solution* as much as it's an experience that needs *compassion*."

—*The Broken Way*, page 241

6. What has this group given you that will help you as you go forward, living and sharing generously as a broken person to be the gift to others?

"The focus of God's people is not to create explanations for suffering, but to create communities around suffering, co-suffering communities to absorb suffering and see it transform into cruciform grace. This will cost us. This will remake us into the image of Christ."

—*The Broken Way*, page 238

7. Read Ann's words above. What would a good co-suffering community being shaped by cruciformity (living broken and given) look like?

"*If I don't fully share my own brokenness . . . there's never full communion?* Maybe—communion can only happen when not only our strong parts are broken and given, but when our broken parts are also given. Maybe communion happens not only when we're broken and given—but *when we give each other our brokenness.*"

—*The Broken Way*, pages 250–251

CLOSING PRAYER

Have a group member read the following paragraphs aloud. Then let everyone share prayer requests. Finally, take time to pray as a group. It's fine for someone to offer a one-sentence prayer or even to pray silently. You may want to focus on thanking God for what you've received from this group.

We have tried to pour ourselves out for others and one another, and we have worked to receive comfort and share our vulnerability. And we've each grown from the experience. This group has strived to be a safe place to share the pain and suffering we have been shaped by. We are deeply grateful to God that Jesus has been our model of giving thanks, breaking, and giving Himself to us. We are grateful for this group and what each person in it has contributed.

We are also eager to offer God the rest of our 25,550 days. We open our hands and lift up to Him these hours and days and weeks, looking forward to His prompting about how we can serve Him through others with our commitment, recognizing each instance of pain we suffer is an opportunity for Him to work through us, to make broken us into a precious gift.

Before we came to this group, we carried our brokenness like a backpack full of bricks. We celebrate those bricks that Jesus has unloaded and put into His own backpack. And we pray to continue surrendering them up to Him to use until we are traveling lighter than we ever have before. Thank you, our dearest Friend, Comforter, and Lord.

FINAL THOUGHTS

Session 6

Work through this section on your own after your discussion of session 6. Ideally, spread out the personal study over several sittings.

You have only begun the journey of living abundantly in and through your brokenness. What does it feel like to begin to live unafraid of broken things, knowing Christ is redeeming everything? In what areas of your life have you begun to refuse to live in fear of brokenness? In this final bit of solo work, you can process and celebrate how far you've come and look ahead to what might be next for you.

MY CELEBRATION

How have you moved forward during this study? Are you less afraid of being broken, or less afraid to tell others about your brokenness? Did you practice givenness in an act of kindness for someone? Do you have an ongoing plan for living given to those you find in need? Are you closer to anyone in your group as a result of this study?

Write down how you've grown. Or if you'd rather sketch, create a picture of how you feel now compared to the way you were when you began the study.

Do something to celebrate your growth. Have a treat; take a bubble bath; go for a long and grateful walk in the woods. Buy yourself some flowers. Make confetti and streamers for a special ceremony. Or take a nap! Do whatever says celebration to you. If you can get your group together for a celebration, or even one other person, go for it.

Finally, send a thank you email to your group facilitator(s). Tell them something they did well, especially anything that made you feel heard, seen, or safe in the group.

MY NEXT STEP

How can you foster a co-suffering community, maybe with people from your group or with others? How can you live not afraid of brokenness?

First, identify one person in your world with whom you suspect you could share a bit of your brokenness. And be a safe person for them to open to. Invite that person to get together with you, or if you naturally encounter them in the course of your week, make a plan to share something genuine when you next meet. Share something more vulnerable than what you usually would.

Who is the person you have in mind, and what might you do?

Next, identify another person in your world to whom you would like to *give* out of your unique brokenness, in a way that you aren't comfortable, that requires you to accept Christ's help to be the gift to them. If it's truly sacrificial, it's an opportunity for transformation to happen. For example, you could:

- Invite someone for coffee or a meal.
- Take flowers to someone.
- Send an "I was just thinking of you" text.

- Visit a sick or elderly relative with them.

- Care for their children.

- Do a household project or yard work for them.

- Whip up a care package or ask to deliver a meal some evening.

- Keep praying daily for the needs shared by group members, and check in with them later for updates.

- Spearhead the outreach project that grows from your research in session 5 into caring for others' needs.

Who is the person you have in mind, and what might you do?

SACRED READING

This final passage for reflection is about abundance. This is where you'll live if you follow God's path of giving and receiving in koinonia. The passage is this:

How priceless is your unfailing love, O God!
People take refuge in the shadow of your wings.

They feast on the abundance of your house;

    you give them drink from your river of delights.

For with you is the fountain of life;

    in your light we see light.

(Psalm 36:7–9)

Who is God in this passage? What is the abundance He offers? What is His river of delights? What is the fountain of life? Think about what all of these images add up to and how they make pictures of abundance that your mind can take in.

Try to sit with this passage for fifteen to twenty minutes. You can do your reflection in any of the following ways:

- You can repeat the passage over and over to yourself, pausing at different words to let them sink in.
- You can pray aloud to God about the passage.
- You can make a sketch that shows what this passage means to you.
- You can journal about the passage, writing about where it takes you and where you find God in it.

As you close your time of reflection, thank God for His abundance, His river of delights, His fountain of life. Thank God that we never have to be afraid of broken things because, in His time, He is making abundance out of everything. Write your prayer below if you'd like. And consider making this practice of sacred reading a regular part of your life in communion with God.

JOURNAL

Journaling can be another practice you take with you going forward. Write today about one of these topics or another of your choosing:

- Offer another brick in your backpack to Jesus.
- Consider how you want to give to others (or maybe to some specific person you are aware of) because of what you've received.
- If you're still reluctant to approach another person with your brokenness, write about what you would say to a friend about your pain if you dared.

"There will be heroes who keep their eyes on the Shepherd, who let the Shepherd and His compassion live in them. That's how He makes real heroes. It's Jesus who fills us up with this light of compassion, with the compassion He's shown us, and we can become heroes, co-sufferers. The heroes are the ones who carry their broken cups of light into the world to leak His healing light. We will bring her His grace, a listening ear, a meal, an invitation to our table, a bunch of wildflowers, we will give her the gift of presence. We will make Christ present, we will be the GIFT, and we will give her cup upon cup of light."

—*The Broken Way*, page 240

The Broken Way

A Daring Path into the Abundant Life

Ann Voskamp

New York Times bestselling author Ann Voskamp sits at the edge of her life and all of her own unspoken brokenness and asks: What if you really want to live abundantly before it's too late? What do you do if you really want to know abundant wholeness? This is the one begging question that's behind every single aspect of our lives—and one that *The Broken Way* rises up to explore in the most unexpected ways.

This one's for the lovers and the sufferers. For those whose hopes and dreams and love grew so large it broke their willing hearts. This one's for the busted ones who are ready to bust free, the ones ready to break molds, break chains, break measuring sticks, and break all this bad brokenness with an unlikely good brokenness. You could be one of the Beloved who is broken—and still lets yourself be loved.

You could be one of them, one who believes freedom can be found not only beyond the fear and pain, but actually within it.

You could discover and trust this broken way—the way to not be afraid of broken things.

Available in stores and online!

One Thousand Gifts

A Dare to Live Fully Right Where You Are

Ann Voskamp

Like most readers, Ann Voskamp hungers to live her one life well. Forget the bucket lists about once-in-a-lifetime experiences.

"How," Ann wondered, "do we find joy in the midst of deadlines, debt, drama, and daily duties? What does a life of gratitude look like when your days are gritty, long, and sometimes dark? What is God providing here and now?

A beautifully practical guide to living a life of joy, *One Thousand Gifts* invites you to wake up to God's everyday blessings. As Voskamp discovered, in giving thanks for the life she already had, she found the life she'd always wanted.

Following Voskamp's grace-bathed reflections on her farming, parenting, and writing life, you will embark on the transformative spiritual discipline of chronicling gifts. You will discover a way of seeing that opens your eyes to gratitude, a way of living so you are not afraid to die, and a way of becoming present to God's presence that brings deep and lasting happiness.

Also available:

One Thousand Gifts available in both blue and brown
  duotone leather editions
*One Thousand Gifts Devotional: Reflections on Finding
  Everyday Grace*
*Selections from One Thousand Gifts: Finding Joy in What
  Really Matters*

One Thousand Gifts Study Guide with DVD

A Dare to Live Fully Right Where You Are

Ann Voskamp with Sherry Harney

In this small group video study, *New York Times* bestselling author Ann Voskamp ponders the question of finding joy in midst of everything from the typical grind of daily chores and deadlines to the catastrophes every person eventually faces.

"How," Ann muses, "do you break the bondage of fear that has white-knuckle control on your life and instead embrace the everyday blessings that immerse you in Christ's fullness? How can you live life with a heart overflowing with delight?"

Ann encourages participants to take on the life-changing discipline of journaling God's gifts—to find the good in life in all circumstances. It's only in this expression of gratitude for the life we already have, that we discover the life we've always wanted ... a life we can take, give thanks for, and use to serve others. In it, we come to feel and know the impossible right down to our core: We are wildly loved by God.

Embark on this personal, honest and fresh exploration of what it means to be deeply fulfilled, wholly happy, and fully alive. When used together, the study guide and companion DVD provide you with a practical tool that can transform your faith.

Sessions include:

1. Attitude of Gratitude
2. Grace in the Moment
3. All Is Grace
4. Trust: The Bridge to Joy
5. Empty to Fill